SUPER SANDCASTLE™
Let's See A to Z

Armpits to Zits

The Body from A to Z

Colleen Dolphin

Consulting Editor, Diane Craig, M.A./Reading Specialist

ABDO
Publishing Company

Published by ABDO Publishing Company, 8000 West 78th Street, Edina, Minnesota 55439. Copyright © 2008 by Abdo Consulting Group, Inc. International copyrights reserved in all countries. No part of this book may be reproduced in any form without written permission from the publisher. Super SandCastle™ is a trademark and logo of ABDO Publishing Company.

Printed in the United States.

Editor: Pam Price
Consulting Editor: Diane Craig, M.A./Reading Specialist
Content Developer: Nancy Tuminelly
Cover and Interior Design and Production: Mighty Media
Photo Credits: 3D4Medicalcom/Getty Images, Image Source, Shutterstock

Library of Congress Cataloging-in-Publication Data

Dolphin, Colleen, 1979-
  Armpits to zits : the body from A to Z / Colleen Dolphin.
    p. cm. -- (Let's see A to Z)
  ISBN 978-1-59928-884-0
  1. Body, Human--Juvenile literature. 2. Human anatomy--Juvenile literature. I. Title.
  QP37.D636 2008
  612--dc22

                    2007005649

Super SandCastle™ books are created by a team of professional educators, reading specialists, and content developers around five essential components—phonemic awareness, phonics, vocabulary, text comprehension, and fluency—to assist young readers as they develop reading skills and strategies and increase their general knowledge. All books are written, reviewed, and leveled for guided reading, early reading intervention, and Accelerated Reader® programs for use in shared, guided, and independent reading and writing activities to support a balanced approach to literacy instruction.

About Super Sandcastle™

Bigger Books for Emerging Readers
Grades PreK–3

Created for library, classroom, and at-home use, Super SandCastle™ books support and engage young readers as they develop and build literacy skills and will increase their general knowledge about the world around them. Super SandCastle™ books are part of SandCastle™, the leading PreK–3 imprint for emerging and beginning readers. Super SandCastle™ features a larger trim size for more reading fun.

Let Us Know

Super SandCastle™ would like to hear your stories about reading this book. What was your favorite page? Was there something hard that you needed help with? Share the ups and downs of learning to read. We want to hear from you! Send us an e-mail.

sandcastle@abdopublishing.com

Contact us for a complete list of SandCastle™, Super SandCastle™, and other nonfiction and fiction titles from ABDO Publishing Company.

www.abdopublishing.com • 8000 West 78th Street Edina, MN 55439 • 800-800-1312 • 952-831-1632 fax

This fun and informative series employs illustrated definitions to introduce emerging readers to an alphabet of words in various topic areas. Each page combines words with corresponding images and descriptive sentences to encourage learning and knowledge retention. AlphagalorZ inspires young readers to find out more about the subjects that most interest them!

The "Guess What?" feature expands the reading and learning experience by offering additional information and fascinating facts about specific words or concepts. The "More Words" section provides additional related A to Z vocabulary words that develop and increase reading comprehension.

These books are appropriate for library, classroom, and home use.

A

Ankles

Ankles connect your feet to your legs.

Ankles let your feet move around.

a

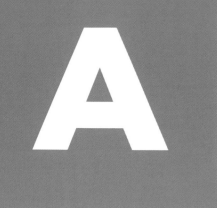

Armpits

Armpits are under your arms.

Your armpits may be very ticklish.

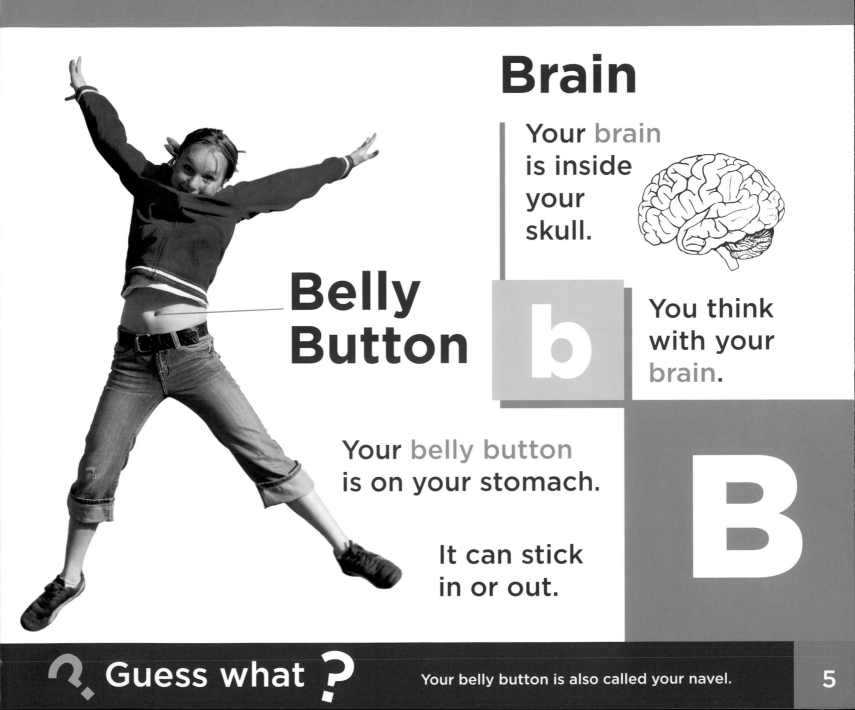

Brain

Your brain is inside your skull.

Belly Button

b

You think with your brain.

Your belly button is on your stomach.

It can stick in or out.

B

Cheeks

Cheeks **are under your eyes.**

Cheeks **are made of bone and muscle.**

Cells

All living things are made of cells.

Cells **make things grow.**

Dream

You have dreams when you are asleep.

Dreams can be strange, happy, or scary.

D
d

A dimple is a small dent on your cheek.

Not everyone has dimples.

Dimple

Eyes

Eyes are organs.

Eyes let us see.

Eyes can blink and wink.

e

Elbows

Elbows are joints.

Elbows let your arms bend.

Elbows hide when your arms are straight.

E

Fingers

Fingers are on your hands.

Fingers let you pick things up and hold them.

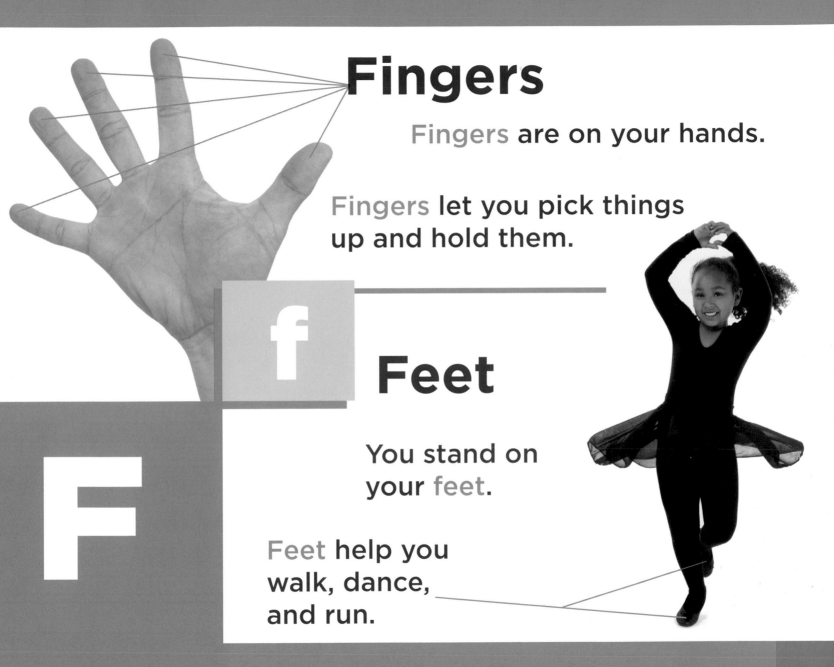

Feet

You stand on your feet.

Feet help you walk, dance, and run.

G g

Gums

Gums are in your mouth.

Your teeth are in your gums.

Giggle

A giggle is a little laugh.

Funny things make you giggle.

Head

Your head has many parts.

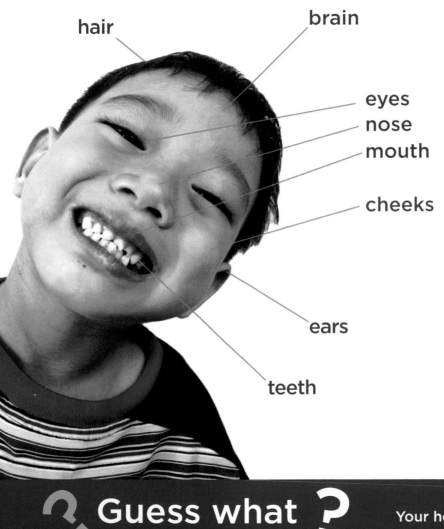

hair

brain

eyes

nose

mouth

cheeks

ears

teeth

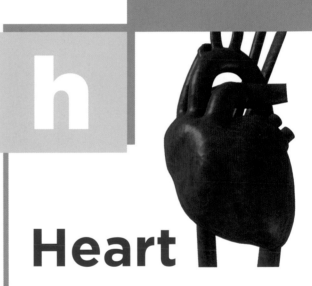

Heart

The heart is a muscle.

It sends blood through your body.

I

Intestines break down your food.

i

Intestines

Intestines are connected to your stomach.

You have a small intestine and a large intestine.

liver

stomach

Guess what ?

The small intestine is about 20 feet long
The large intestine is about 5 feet long.

Joints

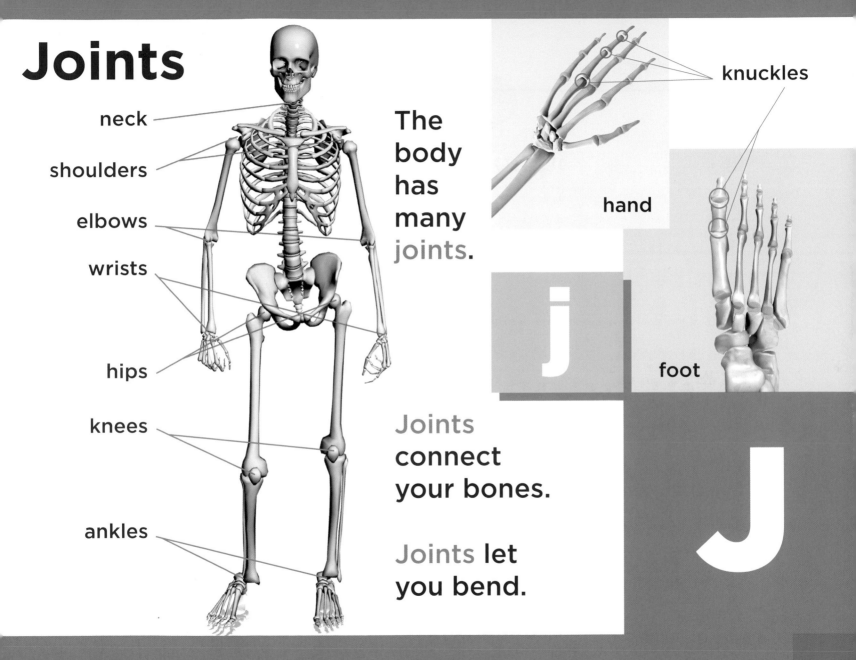

neck

shoulders

elbows

wrists

hips

knees

ankles

The body has many joints.

knuckles

hand

j

foot

Joints connect your bones.

Joints let you bend.

J

Knees

Knees are joints.

Knees let your legs bend.

K

k

Kidneys

Kidneys are behind your intestines and stomach.

Kidneys get rid of waste.

Lungs

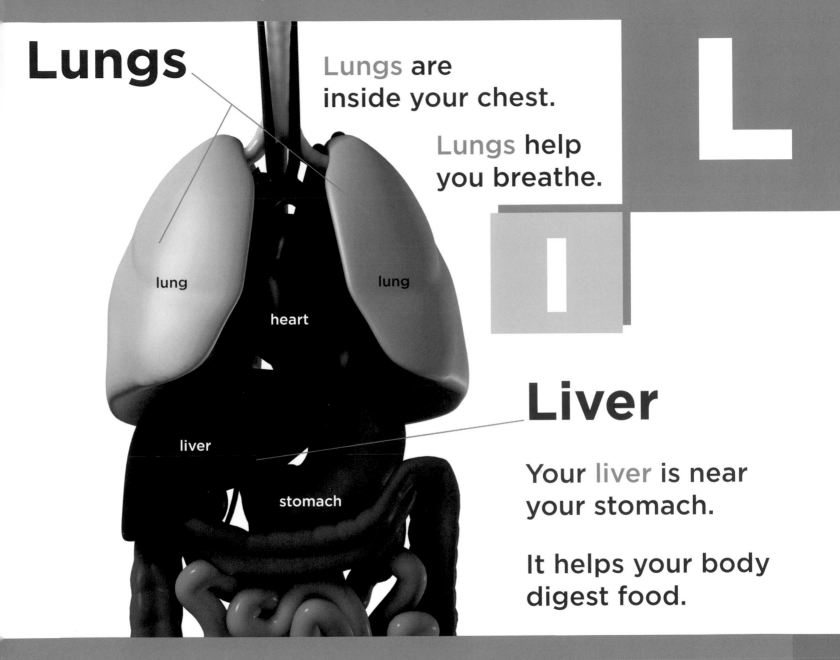

Lungs **are** inside your chest.

Lungs **help** you breathe.

lung

lung

heart

liver

stomach

L

l

Liver

Your liver is near your stomach.

It helps your body digest food.

Mole

A **mole** is a spot on your skin.

Some **moles** feel like bumps.

Muscles

Muscles are in every part of your body.

Muscles help your body move.

Exercise makes your **muscles** strong.

M **m**

Nails

Your nails can scratch an itch.

Nails are on your fingers and toes.

n Nose

Your nose is under your eyes.

Your nose lets you smell and breathe.

N

Oxygen

Oxygen is a gas in the air.

Oxygen cannot be seen.

You need oxygen to breathe.

Trees and plants release oxygen.

Pulse

You can feel your pulse in your wrist.

Your pulse is caused by your heart beating.

You count your pulse to measure how fast your heart is beating.

Quadriceps

Quadriceps **are also called** quads.

Quads **are in your thighs.**

Quadriceps **are a group of four muscles.**

Respiratory System

nose

trachea

lungs

Your nose, trachea, and lungs are part of your respiratory system.

These organs help you breathe.

Spine

Your spine is your backbone.

Your spine goes from your head to your hips.

Food goes into your stomach.

Stomach

Acids in your stomach break down food.

Toes

Toes are on your feet.

Your toes help you balance and walk.

T **t**

Tongue

Your tongue is in your mouth.

You taste things with your tongue.

Urine

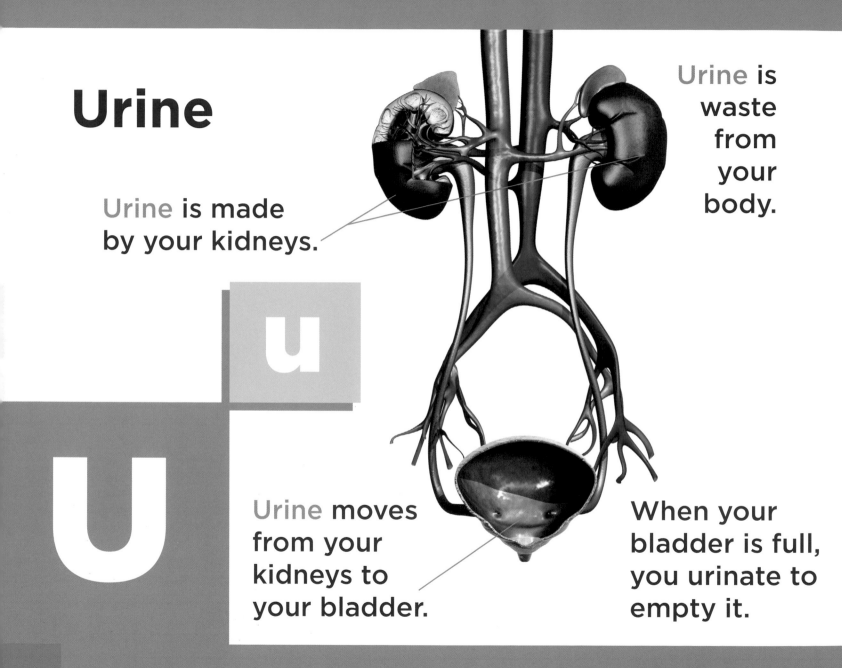

Urine is made
by your kidneys.

Urine is
waste
from
your
body.

U u

Urine moves
from your
kidneys to
your bladder.

When your
bladder is full,
you urinate to
empty it.

Vitamin

Vitamins help you grow and keep you strong.

Fruits and vegetables provide many vitamins.

vitamin D

V

V

vitamins A, C, K

vitamins A, B6, C, E

vitamins A, C, B1

vitamins A, C, E

vitamins A, C

vitamins A, C, K

vitamins A, C, K

vitamins C, K

vitamins A, C

vitamins A, B1, B6, C

W

Wink

You wink when you blink only one eye!

Water

Water is very important for your body.

You should drink water every day!

X-ray

An X-ray is a picture of your bones, lungs, or belly.

X-rays allow doctors to see inside your body.

Y

Yawn

A yawn is a quick, deep breath.

You yawn when you are tired or bored.

Zits

A zit is a red sore on your skin.

A zit is also called a pimple.

Too much oil in your pores causes zits.

Zits last for a short time.

Z

Z

Glossary

bladder – the organ that stores urine.

blink – to quickly shut and open the eyes.

breathe – to inhale and exhale air.

connect – to join two or more things together.

digest – to break down food so the body can use it.

exercise – an activity you do to keep your body healthy and fit.

heartbeat – the cycle in which the heart contracts and relaxes.

itch – a bothersome feeling on the skin.

laugh – a sound you make that lets others know you are happy or amused.

measure – to determine the amount of something.

organ – a body part that does a specific job for the body.

oxygen – a colorless gas found in air, water, and most rocks and minerals.

pore – a small opening in the skin that gas and liquid pass through.

release – to set free or let go.

scratch – to rub or scrape the skin to stop an itch.

skull – the bones that protect the brain and form the face.

sore – a hurt or infected spot on the skin.

ticklish – being likely to laugh or twitch when the skin is touched lightly.

trachea – the tube that carries oxygen to the lungs. The trachea is also called the windpipe.

waste – the leftover material that leaves the body after food is digested.

wrist – the joint between the hand and the arm.

More Body Talk!

Can you learn what these words mean too?

appendix	gall bladder	red blood cell
artery	gene	reflex
back	germ	saliva
blood	gland	shoulder
burp	gluteus maximus	skeleton
calf	hiccup	skin
chest	hip	throat
chin	hormone	tonsil
circulatory system	knuckle	tooth
digestive system	leg	ulcer
ear	lip	uvula
earlobe	mouth	vein
eyebrow	neck	vertebra
eyelash	nostril	virus
eyelid	nutrition	waist
fingerprint	optic nerve	white blood cell
forehead	palm	wisdom tooth
freckle	pancreas	wrist
funny bone	pelvis	zygote